Other books by Melissa Alvarez

Your Color Power
The Writer's Net Anthology of Prose
The Phoenix's Guide To Self Renewal
Paranormal Experiences Volume One
New Age Dimensions Holiday Extravaganza

Writing as Ariana Dupré
Paranormal Romantic Suspense

Night Visions
Talgorian Prophecy
Beneath A Christmas Moon Anthology
Briar Mountain

Featured or quoted in:

Book Marketing A-Z by Francine Silverman
*How To Operate A Successful Pizza & Sub
Restaurant* by Shri Henkel
Successful Meetings by Shri Henkel
Book Marketing 101 by Nikki Leigh

Websites:
www.MelissaA.com
www.APsychicHaven.com

Analyze Your Handwriting

Learn the Basics of Graphology

Melissa Alvarez

Published by

Adrema Press

A NOTICE TO THE READER
LIMIT OF LIABILITY DISCLAIMER OF WARRANTY:

The publisher and author have used their best efforts in preparing this book. The ideas, procedures and suggestions contained in this book are the opinion of the author and are not intended as a substitute for psychological counseling or consultation with your physician. All matters regarding your physical and mental health require medical supervision. The publisher and author make no representations or warranties with any implied warranties of merchantability or fitness for a particular purpose. The accuracy and completeness of the information provided herein and the opinions stated herein are not guaranteed or warranted to produce any particular results and the advice and strategies contained herein may not be suitable for every individual. No warranty may be created or extended by sales representatives or written sales material. Neither the publisher nor author shall be liable for any loss of profit or any other commercial or personal damages, including but not limited to special, incidental, consequential, or other damages. There are no warranties which extend beyond the descriptions contained in this paragraph. The publisher and author assume no liability for damage resulting from this book's information.

Adrema Press, P.O. Box 14592, North Palm Beach, FL 33408
Copyright © 2009 by Melissa Alvarez
ISBN: 978-1-59611-071-7

Library of Congress Control Number: 2009905090

First North American Printing: June 2009
10 9 8 7 6 5 4 3 2 1

Trademarks Acknowledgement

The author acknowledges the trademarked status and trademark owners of the following wordmarks mentioned in this work of non-fiction:

D'Nealian: Scott Foresman, Addison-Wesley Publishing Company
Zaner-Bloser: Zaner-Bloser, Inc.

Author's Notes

The handwriting samples in this book have been reduced to meet formatting requirements. The samples have been created by a graphic designer to imitate actual handwriting styles. This book contains the opinions of the author and is intended as an introduction to the basics of graphology. Sources for more in-depth study are provided in the bibliography. For the sake of consistency, the author uses feminine personal pronouns (she, her, herself) in this text and non-gender specific pronouns (they, their). These terms apply to both males and females.

Contents

Graphology — An Introduction   11
What Graphology Can
    and Cannot Tell You   16
What You Will Need   20
Obtain Writing Samples   24
Handwriting Traits   26
Presence and Size   30
Form — Looking from a Distance   35
Under Pressure   37
Rhythm   42
Where are the Baselines?   44
In the Zone   48
Printing   53
Connections   54
Beginning and Ending Strokes   60
Slants   63
I's and T's   66
Spacing   70
Margins   73
Envelopes   76
Signatures   78
Doodling   87
Composing Your Analysis   92
The Business of Graphology   96
Conclusion   98
Bibliography   99

Graphology – An Introduction

Every person embodies unique characteristics that make each of us different from everyone else on this planet: fingerprints, personalities, hair and eye color, likes and dislikes, fears and dreams, just to name a few. We also have individualized writing styles, which can give others a glimpse into our uniqueness.

I have always been interested in what makes a person tick and how their personality shines through in hidden ways. I enjoy studying body language, eye movements and the slight gestures that people make, which give insight into their character. Usually the information is given away without people realizing it. Either I was a detective in a past life or the policemen in my family impressed upon me the desire to get to the root of behaviors, character traits and personality. Naturally, with my inquisitive nature, I was drawn to understanding character traits and personality through handwriting analysis. Being a clairvoyant, which means I can perceive information and events through the use of abilities beyond the five senses, I use intuition along with analytical skills to understand why people write the way they do and what this says about them on a deeper level.

The analysis of a person's handwriting is referred to as graphology. It has been around since the days of Aristotle and has grown and developed over time into the detailed tool that it is today. Handwriting is the process by which your personality is presented to the world. Graphology is the study of all graphic movement within a given sample of script in order to gain a clear understanding of the mental, emotional and physical states of the writer. Once you know how to read these movements, by studying and using graphology, you will never look at handwriting in the same way again. You will be able to delve into the thoughts, feelings and actions of others simply through handwriting analysis.

Graphology is fun. It is addicting and an intriguing resource that you can use to find out more about the people in your life including friends, family and acquaintances. You can even understand, through handwriting, people you do not know.

Handwriting is often referred to as brainwriting because it is a term that more accurately describes what happens when we put words to paper. Brainwriting reveals who we are and how we behave, think and feel, thus revealing the qualities that are unique to each of us.

When you first learned how to write, you practiced letter creation and perfecting what you were taught in school. Then, as you grew, your writing developed into more than just the standard block style letters. A squiggle here, a loop there—all of these small details in your writing reflect a part of your personality. Once you understand the different meanings associated with handwriting traits, you will be able to tell who is telling the truth and who is lying, who is a hopeless romantic and who is not, who is a loyal person and who will run at the first sign of trouble. With knowledge of graphology, you will be able to tell more than you ever thought possible about people that you may have previously thought you knew well.

While we could get into the technical and medical aspects of how the actual process of writing works, that is not what this book is about. I want to show you how to use graphology to learn more about yourself and those around you but as we do this there are a few things to remember. First, consider this book an introduction to handwriting analysis, a starting point. Then, if what you read here grabs you and you want to know more, then seek out other books that delve into all of the slight nuances of graphology.

Secondly, begin with a sample of your own writing. Take the techniques that I have shared with you and practice on yourself. You will find that there are things that surface during the analysis that may leave you feeling like your secrets have been exposed because your handwriting can show your feelings. If not, then consider having an analysis done by a professional graphologist and this will give you a greater understanding of how it feels to be on the client's side of the analysis. The result could be that a complete stranger knows a lot about you on a deeper level than you may prefer.

As you create a handwriting analysis for someone else, do it with tact and kindness, try not to be blunt and uncaring. Always think of how you would feel in the same situation and consider the other person's feelings. No matter what you think of the graphology process, the fact remains that there is a person behind the handwriting sample that you are analyzing. This person has problems, hopes and dreams just like you do. Their feelings could be injured if you are tactless in your delivery. Put yourself in the client's shoes when you do an analysis.

Graphology is a skill that requires practice.

As you study handwriting analysis, you may review hundreds of samples from many people. The more you practice the better you will become at discovering the hidden information within a person's handwriting.

Most of all have fun analyzing handwriting. It's an interesting and enlightening tool.

What Graphology Can and Cannot Tell You

Graphology can tell you a lot about someone's personality and behavior but it cannot tell you everything. There are limits within the process and you need to know what they are before you start. That way you can present a more accurate report to the person you are working with so that neither of you will have unrealistic expectations going into the analysis.

Graphology cannot tell you a person's age, sex, profession, race/ethnic origin, religion, sexual preference, if she is right-handed or left-handed or anything about her future. Consider these examples:

For instance, say you receive a writing sample that has short harsh strokes with pointy letters. You may assume this is a man's handwriting when in fact it is an angry woman. Or maybe there are lots of wide loops in the sample—a woman right? Not necessarily, this could just as well be a man's writing sample. Do not expect graphology to tell you the person's gender or sexual preference. It does not show either.

As we mature, so does our writing. Sometimes though, a person's emotional status is much younger than her physical age. Handwriting that looks like it should belong to an eighty year old man may actually belong to a forty year old woman or vice versa. So while you will be able to see the person's maturity level through the writing, you will not be able to see the actual age.

It is also a common misconception that if a person's writing slants to the left, she is left-handed and if it slants to the right, she is right-handed. This is false because graphology cannot show which hand a person writes with. In fact, it is quite common that left-handed writers do not have writing that slants to the left.

Maybe you have a sample that is boxy with little or no extraneous marks. You might think that a white Presbyterian woman wrote this when it fact it was a black male Baptist or a Catholic Latin woman. How can you tell? The fact is, you cannot.

These types of criteria are not shown in graphology and it is important to be clear about the limitations of the profession prior to beginning your own analysis. Let go of any preconceived notions you may be harboring about what is "typical" handwriting for a certain type of person.

What *can* graphology tell you? Let us start with what graphology can do for you on a personal level. It can give you an accurate means to understanding your own personality and character traits. You may even discover certain realizations that you have hidden from yourself while uncovering your strengths and weaknesses. You can utilize the information that you have discovered to work on yourself to obtain more balance within your life on many levels. You can use this information to choose a career, understand your health and develop a keener understanding of the kind of person you want to be versus the kind of person you are.

Next, graphology can help you understand others better as well. It can clue you in to the moods, the core personality and specific character traits of those around you. If you want to get along with someone better, take a look at their handwriting. You may discover that they have hidden fears that are causing them to put up walls. If that is the case then you can determine the best way to approach them to help bring down those walls.

Lastly, it can also give you a good look into your compatibility with someone else whether you are involved with them on a personal level, in business or merely as a casual acquaintance. By doing a comparative analysis of your handwriting with theirs, you will find similarities and differences that will give you indications as to how you will get along.

What You Will Need

There are a few tools that you will need as you delve into the world of graphology. The first is knowledge. Once you start doing handwriting analysis you may decide you like doing it for fun or you may decide that you would like to do it professionally. If the career route is the one you would like to take, there are a few schools of graphology available or you can learn from someone who is a professional instructor in the field.

A basic understanding of psychology and the development of the human personality will help you with handwriting analysis. Graphology is primarily a way to describe personality as expressed through the written text. A lack of basic understanding of human personality and psychology will inhibit your ability to give a detailed analysis. If you already have this knowledge then you are ahead of the learning curve. If not, take a class or two, read some books and do research into the basics of psychology and personality. Apply this information in conjunction with what you have learned about handwriting in your analysis. Using your own intuition is also important so do not discard your gut feelings. Look closely to see if you can find evidence in the written words to back up what you are sensing about the writer.

You will need several mechanical tools at your disposal. A ruler that has millimeters (which is the best unit of measurement to use during the analysis) is used to measure margins and baselines, a protractor is used to measure slant and a good magnifying glass will show you small intricacies within the writing sample. These items can be picked up at any store that sells school supplies. The magnifying glass should be able to magnify the sample two to five times larger than normal and should be wide enough to give you a good view.

You will also need a standard to measure against. A copybook is the common standard of the alphabet that you learned in school. Writing was previously taught using copybooks, which is when you copy the text from the copybook onto your own paper. This taught the student to write according to the standard used at that time. As a person matures, their writing changes to reflect their own feelings and personality but in graphology you still compare the adult writer's text against copybook standards.

Think back to grade school and the

alphabet posters that the teacher always had on the wall. This is a standard that was used to teach children to form letters matching the copybook. The Palmer, Zaner-Bloser or the D'Nealian methods are generally taught in the United States. If the person you are analyzing was in school prior to 1980 you will want to use the Palmer or Zaner -Bloser standards. If they were in school after 1980 use the D'Nealian method as a comparison because the standard methods taught in school changed around 1980. It is a good idea to keep a copy of all three copybook standards in your work materials. If you live outside of the United States you should find out what is considered the common standard of handwriting in your country and use those copybooks for the measurements. Here are basic examples of the three prominent copybooks used in the United States.

Palmer Copybook Example:

ABCDEFGHIJKLMNOPQRSTUVWXYZ

abcdefghijklmnopqrstuvwxyz 1 2 3 4 5 6 7 8 9 0

Zaner-Bloser Copybook Example:

ABCDEFGHIJKLMNOPQRSTUVWXYZ
abcdefghijklmnopqrstuvwxyz 1234567890
ABCDEFGHIJKLMNOPQRSTUVWXYZ
abcdefghijklmnopqrstuvwxyz 1234567890

D'Nealian Copybook Example:

ABCDEFGHIJKLMNOPQRSTUVWXYZ
abcdefghijklmnopqrstuvwxyz 1234567890
ABCDEFGHIJKLMNOPQRSTUVWXYZ
abcdefghijklmnopqrstuvwxyz 1234567890

Obtain Writing Samples

As you start to delve into the study of graphology, you will need to gather writing samples. Start with your own handwriting sample and then move on to samples from family members and friends. You will want to get a variety of spontaneous samples if possible. Try to obtain the handwriting when the person is in different moods. A sample obtained when the person is happy will give a different analysis than one obtained when the person is sad, tired or frustrated.

If you cannot obtain samples from people when they are in different moods, then you can create your own mood samples. Create a sample when you are relaxed, energetic and so on. Remember to make notes of the mood and attach it to the sample (so you do not forget). Then you can compare them against one another to find out more about yourself.

Try to get the best possible handwriting sample that you can obtain. The perfect handwriting sample will consist of original writing on unlined paper — the more text the better — written with any type of ink pen on a smooth hard surface by someone who is not under the influence of alcohol, drugs or heavy medication.

Let the person choose what they would like to write about instead of giving them text to copy. Their subject matter can sometimes be insightful when doing your analysis even though it is not a component of graphology. Do not require the person to print or write in cursive. Let them write in their natural handwriting. You will find that some people use a combination of both printing and cursive, commonly referred to as printscript by graphologists.

Obtain basic information about the person giving you the sample, including their age, gender, if they are on medication or have had any problems that could affect their handwriting.

The longer the writing sample, the more you will be able to understand the hidden personality and character traits of that writer. There will be more opportunity for small details to show during a longer sample. So, while you should always aim for one page, if someone wants to write ten pages, then let them write it. Always remember to get the author to sign their handwriting sample. Signatures can give you a lot of information into the person's character in a different way from the overall analysis.

Handwriting Traits

There are many traits, which are distinguishing features within a person's handwriting, associated with conducting an analysis. As you are doing the analysis you will look for several of them that mean the same thing before declaring that the person has the characteristic associated with the writing trait. Some to look for are imaginative, honest, caring and loyal. Once a trait appears several times then you can make a well founded decision that the person does indeed embody the accompanying characteristic.

You will want to look at these traits in two distinct ways. First consider the overall picture of the sample as a whole and consider characteristics that could be associated with the manner of writing. Then look at each individual trait (slant, margins, letter size and so on), one at a time, to see what each one means in the grand scheme of the analysis.

When you look at the overall picture, you will want to consider some of the following traits:

- Is the writing neat or sloppy?
- How does the writer fill the page?
- Are the margins large or small?
- Does the text slant to the right or left?
- Does it flow up or down?
- Is there a slant to the base line?
- Are the letters round or square?
- Are the words large and full of loops or small and tight?
- Does the text have extraneous marks?

Now consider each individual trait.

- In which direction does each letter slant?
- Does the slant change on any particular word?
- Is the letter size consistent or does it change from word to word?
- Is the lettering tight or loose?
- Is the spacing even or erratic between words?

Consider the following examples. Pick the sample of the person who is sick of their job.

A. *My job is fabulous!*

B. *My job is fabulous!*

Did you pick B? Then you chose correctly. Look at the word job in the second example. Notice how the slant changes to the left instead of the right? This change in slant shows that the person who wrote this is withdrawing from thoughts of her job. Could this be because the company has been sold and the employee is unsure of her job security? Or maybe it is because she dislikes the job and is ready to move to something new. For whatever reason, this change in slant is showing dissatisfaction in her job.

Here is another example of someone who writes that she is excited to be somewhere. Do you think she is really excited or wishes she was somewhere else?

I'm so *excited* to be here.

Take a look at the word "excited". Notice how it leans to the right and the letters are a little closer together? This indicates that she really is excited to be where she is. You can almost see her excitement through the subtle changes in the way the word excited was written.

Next we will take a look at some of the most common traits graphologists consider when conducting a handwriting analysis.

Presence and Size

What is presence? It is the energy you radiate that lets others around you know the quality or manner of your persona. Pretend we are at a party and you are standing near the door looking at the people attending. See the guy who seems to just fill the room? Everyone stops to speak to him. He is drawing everyone's attention without even trying. This man seems to radiate a quiet, confident self-assurance. Now look around the perimeter of the room. See the woman sitting at the table alone? Jotting down something on a notepad as she sips tea? She smiles and speaks to people walking by? She is projecting a presence of poised practicality. Now check out the guy near the punch bowl who steps back every time anyone comes close to him. He is exhibiting uneasiness with being at the party. These people all have a different presence, which would also be reflected in their handwriting.

Now pretend that you obtained a handwriting sample from each of these people. Here are samples of what each may look like. Can you choose which one belongs to each of the three people you noticed?

This is a great party.
I'm glad you invited me.

A.

This is a great party.
I'm glad you invited me.

B.

This is a great party.
I'm glad you invited me.

C.

So, who is who? If you think that the guy drawing all of the attention at the party is A then you are correct. This is an example of large writing. The overall picture of the sample is big and each letter is tall and wide with a bit of flamboyancy. People who write with large letters tend to like to be in the center of any situation. They are confident, bold, self-reliant and have high self-esteem. They are open to new ideas and usually make an impression on those they come into contact with. They are not easily forgettable and usually have jobs that put them in the public eye. Individuals with large handwriting can be too generous, which is a good thing if you are on the receiving end, and extravagant. This keeps the attention on them. On the other hand, they can be easily sidetracked, smug, boastful, arrogant, tactless and vague. Their focus is on themselves and what they are doing more than it is on what others think and feel or what is going on around them. If a person's handwriting is overly large then she possesses these same traits but to a deeper degree.

Which partygoer do you think writing sample B belongs to? If you picked the guy by the punch bowl, you are right again. This is an example of small writing. The overall picture is small with the letters placed close together, in a compact organized way. People who write small are realists who prefer privacy. They do not want everyone knowing their business. They are objective when looking at things and logical in their approach to problems. They are "brainiacs" with a tendency to be overly analytical. They can sometimes put limits on themselves which hold them back and may feel inhibited or inferior to others. They tend to pay attention to what others say even though they may be a bit shy and try to avoid social interaction. Have you ever noticed that your doctor's handwriting is small? Many doctors, scientists, programmers, and others who deal with facts, figures or research have small handwriting that is sometimes very difficult to read. If a person's handwriting is overly small then these traits are intensified within her.

That only leaves the third sample, which will have to belong to the woman sitting at the table working while speaking to others. Writing sample C is an example of medium-sized writing or what is considered "normal" sized writing. People who have this presence in their writing are usually very flexible and adapt well to different situations, emergencies or having extra work thrown their way. They often show good judgment and approach life with a sense of practicality. They are team players who are well balanced and can handle a lot of things at once, are organized and tend to be leaders rather than followers. They are social people who others deem to be trustworthy based upon their actions. A strong sensibility is often seen in people whose handwriting is medium-sized. But they can sometimes be nosy and judgmental or come on too strong. On average, most people write within the normal range but can write larger or smaller depending upon mood and other factors that may be affecting them.

Presence is one of the first things you will want to look at as you consider the big picture of the handwriting sample you are analyzing.

Form – Looking from a Distance

Form is the overall impression that you receive from the handwriting sample as you begin your analysis. You will look at the work as a whole and on a large scale before you look at the individual details just as a scientist would look at a leaf as a whole before putting it under the microscope. It is this large scale that is the "form" of the sample – the overall things that you see before you dig into the deeper layers of the individual words and lettering.

Once the eye is trained and you have experience in doing an analysis you will be able to tell a variety of things when looking at the sample as a whole unit instead of the individual words. You will be able to detect the writer's personality and maturity level as well as their intelligence.

You will also want to look at the sample as if it is a picture. Take a sample of your own writing and put it against your computer screen, tape it to the wall or prop it up against something else and then take a few steps back. What is the first thing you notice?

Do you notice the margins? The slant to

the work as a whole? We will get more into margins and slants further in this book but the way the person uses the page and how they fill it, including whether or not their paragraphs are slanted up or down or not at all will offer insights into their personality.

Before you look at the unique traits within the text make sure you look at the text as a whole before you start the analysis.

Under Pressure

How hard do you write? Do you have a tight grip on the pen and really press down to get a bold stroke on the page? Or do you hold the pen gently and without pressure so that your text is very light? Most of us fall somewhere in the middle range. The amount of pressure that is used can also be affected by mood and energy level. You may press harder when you are emotional or in a hurry and lighter if you are relaxing by the fire.

There are three basic types of pressures important in handwriting analysis—heavy, medium and light. Each of these pressure levels gives us insights into the character of a person. While one person may not have all of the characteristics that a specific trait indicates, it is important to consider the options during an analysis. Let us take a look at all three to determine what they can tell us.

Heavy pressure is when a person really presses down on the page. Here is an example of heavy pressure:

I thought you knew.

What can you learn from someone who uses heavy pressure in their writing? First and foremost it reveals the energy level at the time that the sample was given. What characteristics do people who write with heavy pressure embody? They tend to be serious, more critical, opinionated and quick to react to situations. They can be aggressive, forceful, egotistical and seek material success. They gravitate toward the social scene, partying and things in excess. They like to work with their hands. These are very intense people who sometimes do not know when to stop. The heavier the pressure the more intense these characteristics tend to show within the personality, especially anger and frustration. Heavy pressure also points to high stress levels.

When a writing sample shows medium pressure, it is an indicator that the writer is well balanced, grounded and less energetic than the writer who uses heavy pressure. They are dependable, reliable and have the ability to follow through in difficult situations and times of stress. These are people who do not go to extremes but tend to take the middle ground. They are able to look at both sides of a situation prior to making a decision and consider all options. They are more open-minded and do not lose their temper often. Of the three types of pressure used in handwriting, medium is the most prevalent in society. Here is an example of medium pressure:

Meet me downtown at 3.

Light pressure has a fainter appearance because the person writing is putting very little weight on the page. Here is an example:

What do you mean?

A person who writes with light pressure is on the opposite end of the spectrum from a person who uses heavy pressure. They tend to stay away from the spotlight and any kind of conflict or problems because they are more sensitive than most. They tend to tire easily, may be frail and sickly or very emotional. They can get their feelings hurt easily. Most dislike arguments but they can be overly critical and quickly offended. These tend to be highly spiritual people who are shy, modest and sensitive to those around them. While not weaklings, they do not have as much vitality as a writer who uses medium or heavy pressure. Extremely light pressure results in words that can barely be seen on the page and usually means that the person is depressed or overwhelmed with life and often keeps to themselves in quiet environments.

Pressure can sometimes be evident in the up, down and horizontal strokes within the writing sample. When pressure is appearing in a place that it should not be, then this tells the graphologist that the author of the sample is displacing her feelings. Maybe the person is excitable and seems to be hyper most of the time, yet the displaced pressure tells a different story. On the inside, the person may be unsure and lack confidence, so she presents herself in a different way to cover her own insecurities. Or maybe the opposite is true and the person is calm and confident on the outside but bursting at the seams on the inside. She may be afraid to really let go and be herself because of preconceived notions of how she should behave.

When conducting an analysis, always note whether or not the pressure is well balanced within the text or if it is heavier in places where it should not appear (as in the crossing of the letter t or a long final stroke at the end of the word) because these will clue you in to the fact that this person has something different going on inside that is in contradiction to the appearance she is offering to the public.

Rhythm

The rhythm in a handwriting analysis shows the graphologist an overview of the writer's physical, mental and spiritual self, her self-control, and willpower. In order to decide if the handwriting sample you are analyzing is rhythmic or out of rhythm you will need to look for specific traits.

Rhythmic writing shows harmony and balance within a person's life. The traits that you will look for are even spacing between the letters, a medium pressure, upward and downward strokes that are about the same height, and balance between the size of the letters. Rhythmic samples are usually obtained from people who are consistent, intelligent and have good control over their emotions. Here is an example of rhythmic writing:

When you get to the airport come to the bottom level. I'll come around and pick you up. I drive a black van.

Writing that is out of rhythm shows a lack of harmony and balance within a person's life. These samples will have varying slants within the script, large gaps between the letters and words and fluctuations in the pressure used upon the page. People who write out of rhythm are quite often emotionally intense, impulsive, creative, artistic and seem to have drama in their lives. They can be restless, anxious and easily distracted. Here is writing that is out of rhythm:

I don't care what you think. I can do whatever I want. YOU have no control over me.

Where are the Baselines?

Imagine a lined sheet of paper. You are supposed to write each word straight across and on the line right? This line is considered the baseline in handwriting analysis. When you obtain your writing samples, you will always want to have the subjects write on unlined paper so you can see how they create their own individual baselines when they do not have a printed line to follow. It is difficult for most people to write in a straight line without a printed line being on the page. The slight slants up or down are instrumental in doing an analysis.

Baselines can tell us a number of things about someone depending upon its rise or fall. There are four main types of baselines considered in graphology. These are straight, upward, downward and erratic.

With a straight baseline you will discover that the writer is a reliable person with common sense and good control of her willpower. She is not easily distracted, is able to find ways around problems and quick resolutions to situations without falling apart. She is goal-oriented and responsible. This is an example of a straight baseline:

Are you walking around the lake or riding your bike to the park?

When considering both the upward and downward baselines you need to consider how much it slants up or down.

Look at the upward slope first. If there is only a slight upward tilt to the baseline then the writer is probably sure of herself, confident in her abilities and optimistic. This writer does not let her emotions get the best of her but instead keeps a calm and focused outlook on life. If the upward slant to the baseline is extreme then this shows someone who feels that life is an uphill struggle and that she always has to work harder and harder to get ahead. This type of person may also be easily excitable and emotional. This example is of a slight upward slope.

Here's five dollars. Can you get some chips and soda when you go to the store?

With a downward baseline, you will often find that the person is ill or has recently gone through a major life trauma, such as a death in the family, a divorce or job loss. If none of these are true for the person then it indicates that she has a negative outlook on life. The deeper the baseline slopes downward, as in the sample below, the more intense the feelings. When you see a deeply downward sloping baseline, she is not motivated or enthusiastic about life and tends to give up easily. She may be depressed and despondent.

Tell me a story about a bunny, a turtle and a dove. Make it happy, sad and fun.

An erratic baseline has a wavy appearance. When you see this type of baseline in a writing sample you have someone who just cannot make up her mind and when she does, she is inclined to change her mind quickly. She avoids conflict like the plague, tends to be moody and wander aimlessly through life. The more wavy the baseline the more these traits are accentuated. The writer with an extremely erratic baseline will drop everything and everyone if something or someone better comes along. This individual is often seen as insincere, flighty, emotionally unstable and unpredictable. You cannot depend on this type of person because they may or may not follow through with previously made plans. More often than not, she will let you down.

The sun was shining down on the crytal white sand. I strode along the sandy beach wondering what to do.

In the Zone

When you start analyzing the individual aspects of a handwriting sample, there are three zones that will clue you in to specific personality and character traits inherent to each individual zone. These three zones are the lower, middle and upper. The more a person tends to write within a zone, the more the character and personality traits associated with that zone are accentuated in the person giving the sample.

Imagine three bars. The first contains the main body of the letters making up a word. This is the middle zone. The second contains all of the loops and lines above the main body of the word. This is the upper zone. The third contains all the loops and lines below the main body of the word. This is the lower zone. Here is what the three zones look like. The word strong in this example makes good use of all three zones and is balanced.

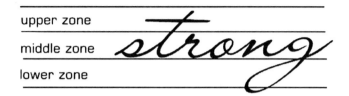

Now take a look at each specific zone, the letters and traits associated with it and a writing sample that emphasizes each zone.

The first zone we will consider is the middle because it contains the biggest portion of the text. The letters that fill the middle zone are a, c, e, m, n, o, r, s, u, v, w, x and sometimes z. This zone tells us about the person's ego and how she reacts to and balances her everyday life.

The middle zone writer does not use long or tall lettering that falls into the other two zones. The lines are short and remain close to the middle zone. These people live for the moment, for today, in the now. People who tend to write primarily within the middle zone are trying to make an impression on others. They like to be the center of attention and the more their writing is forced within this middle section the more pronounced these traits can be, making them selfish, domineering and careless about the results of their actions. They can be egotistical and childlike (think of an adult throwing a temper tantrum) and find waiting for things in life difficult.

The lower zone contains the letters j, p, q, y and sometimes z. The letter F also falls into this zone as well as the upper zone. It is the only letter of the alphabet that can cross all three zones in both print and cursive writing. This zone shows you the writer's materialism, physical and sexual drive, instincts and desires, and interest in sports. The lower zone is reflective of the lower body and libido. This section really embodies the person's id and what they feel on a primitive level; it is what drives them. When writers stay within the lower zone more than any other, they are driven to "keep up with the Joneses". They are hard workers who put great importance in having material possessions and making great achievements in their lives. If they do not meet the standards that they have set for themselves, they consider themselves failures. They tend to be obsessive in one or more areas such as their body image, material possessions, family or those they love, money, sex, success and career. This does not mean they are limited to those specific areas because they can tend to obsess about anything.

When the strokes are so long that they go into the upper or middle level of the words on the line below it, this shows that these people, while striving to achieve their goals, have a lack of judgment when making decisions. Their lives may seem chaotic and they do not seem to think with clear logic. These are people who always seem to have some kind of drama happening in their lives and appear to feed off of that drama. Triangular loops often suggest that the person is sexually frustrated, argumentative and has a short fuse. They tend to be rash and impulsive with strong opinions. The longer this triangular loop, the stronger these tendencies.

hopping

The final zone is the upper zone. The associated letters are b, d, f, h, k, l, and t. This zone identifies the writer's superego, mind, consciousness, thinking self, hopes and dreams. Someone who primarily stays in this zone when she writes tends to be meditative, seeking perfection and living in her imagination. She can be very religious, creative and idealistic. She often lacks practicality and can have problems with every day life. The more prominent the lettering in the upper zone, the more of a dreamer and idealist she will be. She can be less ambitious and more satisfied with the run of the mill lifestyle preferring to live a fantasy life in her mind. She chooses theory and "what if" over realism.

Printing

There are several reasons why someone may choose to print instead of using cursive writing in her day-to-day life. Her handwriting may be difficult to read, she may be required to print because of her job, she may not want to reveal herself to others or she does not really want to say what she is writing.

Printing can utilize all three zones with the exception of block printing, which primarily stays within the middle zone. During your analysis of the writing, you will consider the use of zones just like you would in cursive writing. Print that stays in the upper zone is going to indicate a dreamer and idealist. If it stays primarily in the middle zone then the ego rules.

Sometimes a person combines printing and cursive in what graphologists refer to as printscript, which can mean that she is creative or unpredictable depending on how the overall picture of the sample comes together. Here is an example of printscript.

Can we go to the movies?

Connections

When we talk about connections in handwriting analysis we are talking about the way an individual joins together the letters of each word as she writes them. There are six basic ways that a writer makes these connections and, depending on how she does it, we can learn a lot about her personality. These six types of connections are known as angular, garland, copybook, wavy, thread and arcade.

Within each of these connections there are two more elements that we need to consider. Are the letters actually connected and linked together or are they disconnected with open spaces between each letter? And how can you tell? Let us examine examples of both linked and disconnected writing.

If the letters join together and the script does not have a break from one letter to another, this is connected writing. Look at the s in store in the example below. Notice how the s does not connect to the t. That is a small example of disconnected writing within the sentence. This could mean that the writer had a momentary lapse in concentration at that point in time. Maybe someone interrupted her or the phone rang but she finished the sentence before answering it.

I'm going to the store to get a new hat.

A connected writer consistently joins together each letter within a word. She is adaptable, reliable and social. She has good reasoning skills, can remember a lot of information and is often a deductive thinker. She can sometimes appear superficial or inconsiderate to others. She tends to make quick decisions.

If several letters are joined but there is a break and then more letters join, this is known as disconnected writing as in the next examples below. In disconnected writing, usually only three letters connect before there is a break. The first sentence shows each letter disconnected from the next. This is an extreme example of disconnected writing. The second sentence is what you are more likely to encounter during an analysis.

The store has new hats.
Little shells cluttered the coast line.

Disconnected writing shows us that the writer is lacking in concentration. This type of person tends to listen to her gut instincts and pays close attention to detail, sometimes to the point that she misses the big picture. She cannot see the forest for the trees. She can be moody and stubborn. She does not plan ahead, is very cautious and individualistic. Disconnected writers are often original thinkers, inventors, artists, and musicians.

In angular handwriting, the strokes are firm, controlled and can be rigid. The strokes may even have a pointy and extremely vertical appearance. Angular writing shows that the person can be argumentative, uncompromising and does not adapt well to her environment. An angular writer can be a hard individual who follows her head and can be quite ruthless in dealing with others. She thinks that giving in or adapting to situations where she is the one that needs to make a change, is showing weakness and this she will not do. Those who use angular connection in their writing can be stubborn, intolerant and lack a sense of humor.

This is a sample of my handwriting.

Garland connections are usually found in women's handwriting but the gender cannot be counted on. You may also find men who use garlands in their writing. The script often looks as if it is made up of only lowercase lettering, which gives each letter a bowl like appearance. People who use garland connections are usually good listeners who are responsive to those around them and sympathetic to the needs of others. These people are not argumentative and tend to stay away from conflict. Sometimes they may be indecisive and can be a bit lazy at times.

We could wear jeans to the show.

Copybook connections are what you learn in elementary school. Writers who still use copybook connections as adults are those that are predictable conformists and who feel safest when staying on the beaten path. She will stay away from risks and chance. She tends to be a follower instead of a leader, uneducated instead of educated, and secretive instead of open. This type of connection can also suggest that she is a criminal or has the potential to become a criminal. It is difficult to motivate someone who uses copybook connections. She would prefer to let someone else do the work and take care of her while she just muddles along in life.

Mister Johnson isn't at home.

Wavy connections look just like the description—wavy. The letters appear to disintegrate into little bumps or waves. Pay particular attention to the u, r, n's, and m's in the example below. They are formed by a series of tiny "waves" instead of clearly defined lettering. These writers tend to be laid-back, freedom-loving individuals who avoid commitment (in everything). She may tell lies to get what she wants. On the other hand she can be very diplomatic when dealing with others. She prefers her life to be without obligations or responsibilities.

You're certainly good at mimicking a monkey.

Thread connections are thin and ghostly with the ends of words trailing off into what looks like threads, thus the name. Someone who uses thread connections is quite often clever, versatile, influential and intuitive. She can be manipulative and shirk off responsibility. She may work as an artist, in theatre or any other field that is considered "the arts". She has lots of creativity and talent, is very observant and optimistic.

Can you pass the salt?

Arcade handwriting looks like a series of arches. Its appearance is the opposite of garland connections. Those who use arcade connections have strong creative streaks. She can be hard to get to know by projecting a formality and aloof presence to cover shyness. This type of connection is quite often found in the writing of musicians. She feels emotions deeply and does not trust others much, even if you are her friend.

Meet me in the mountains.

Beginning and Ending Strokes

When you analyze a handwriting sample it is imperative that you look at the beginning and ending strokes of words because they will tell you if the person prepares herself before starting a task or project and whether or not she will finish it. There are several different types of strokes that you will need to be familiar with to do an analysis.

Quite often a handwriting sample will not have an initial stroke on the letters. When a writer does not include initial strokes, she tends to be flexible and easily adapts to any situation. She is positive, outgoing and does not tend to make a big deal over things. Most people who do not use an initial stroke are leaders who think outside of the box.

run away from here

A long initial stroke is indicative of a person who makes endless preparations prior to starting a project and will see it through to the end and then some. These writers can be very active and involved with many things at once. With the long initial stroke you will also need to consider the speed at which the text is written. The slower the speed, the lower her mental capacities are. The faster the speed the more active and involved she is in her life.

boy you're pretty bizarre.

When a word begins with a hook stroke, it is showing someone who is persistent and can tend to have an angry outlook on life. She firmly maintains her opinions and it is nearly impossible to change her mind.

Hello. First time here?

If a person has the initial stoke even with the baseline then this indicates a nervous personality with an inferiority complex especially if she is asked to make a decision. The bigger the decision the more upset she becomes. She is often a conformist who would rather be delegated to than have to be the one doing the delegating.

better make water

Feeling strokes are similar to long initial strokes in that the person must prepare before she writes. With the feeling stroke, it looks more like an extra mark or doodle at the beginning of the letter and shows a lack of confidence in the individual.

My name is Mary.

Ending strokes can show a variety of things about a person. Most people will end their words with anything from a long stroke to a short stroke or even a backward stroke. When a writer uses a long stroke it shows her to be outgoing. If the word stops suddenly, she tends to be boring and stuffy. If she uses a backward stroke she can be aggressive or unemotional.

One for the money

Slants

There are three types of slants that are investigated during a handwriting analysis. These are the left slant, the vertical slant and the right slant. Each reveals something different about the writer. Some writers also use varying slants in their text and that is revealing too.

The left slant belongs to a shy and reserved daydreamer. This is someone who does not openly participate in group conversations but instead prefers to listen...and she is an amazing listener with good shoulders to cry on. She does not expect others to do things for her but relies only on herself. She is a private person who respects the privacy of others. She is observant and cautious. She finds it hard to deal with changes in her life and quite often has a dominant parent or other person in her childhood that suppressed her. She is sentimental, tender and devotes herself fully to causes that are important to her. Someone who has a left slant to her writing can be afraid of committing to one person, to a career or project. She may be insincere and selfish. A left slant also indicates a fear of the future, a tendency to be too cautious and a lack of spontaneity.

Remember that a left or right slant does not indicate that the person is left- or right-handed. Handedness cannot be discovered through graphology.

Lilacs and petunias smell wonderful.

The vertical slant belongs to an independent, extroverted person who is reasonable, analytical and who has good self-control. She is a self-sufficient leader who can maintain a balanced outlook on life without getting emotionally wrapped up in situations. It is easy for her to be neutral and she makes a good mediator. She looks for logical reasons and facts. When someone uses a vertical slant it indicates an overall calm neutral attitude and a poised, dignified person who relies upon herself. She may be cautious and reserved but has amazing focus and concentration. Sometimes she can come across as critical and indifferent with a pessimistic outlook on life. You may even think of her as conceited and boring.

Call me soon!

The right slant is the way most of us write. Someone who slants her writing to the right tends to be friendly and outgoing. She looks forward to and plans for the future. She is sociable, spontaneous and enthusiastic about life. She has the ability to cope with just about any situation thrown in front of her and does not try to hide her feelings. A large slant to the right indicates that she may also be more emotional, impulsive and irresponsible than someone with a slighter slant.

You'll never know why I did it.

When a writer varies her slant between the left, vertical and right, then she is versatile and active. She can adapt easily to changes in her life, is intelligent, outgoing and friendly. However, a stronger varying slant is also indicative of someone who is unpredictable, has mood swings or is unstable. Writers using a variable slant are very indecisive and restless.

Today is monday June 3rd.

I's And T's

When considering the lowercase letter i and t, you are going to look at the way the person dots her i's and crosses her t's. The way this is carried out reveals different things, so make sure you look closely at both of these two letters individually and how they connect and relate to the rest of the letters in the word. With both the lowercase i and t, there are three specific things you are going to look for:

- Is it placed high or low in relation to the stem?
- Does it have rightward or leftward movement?
- What is its location?

We will look at the lowercase i first. Here are the most common placements of the dot over the i and what they reveal about the writer.

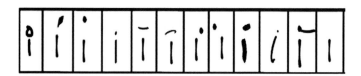

Dot looks like a circle	Shows a sense of humor
Pointy dot	Aggressive, sarcastic, mean
Dot is central and high	A dreamer, nosy
Dot is central and low	Detail-oriented, great memory, not creative
Horizontal line dot	Sensitive, impressionable, critical, often feels slighted
Arc dot	Excellent observer with a vivid imagination
Dot to right of stem	Practical and reserved, goal-oriented
Dot to left of stem	Cautious, ponders situations, hesitant
Heavy dot to right	Restless, impatient, under stress
Light dot	Apathetic and without energy
Dot connected to next letter	Quick thinker, smart, with a positive outlook on life
No dot	Sloppy, a quick thinker

Now let us look at the most common characteristics of the lowercase t and what they mean in handwriting analysis.

Bar low on stem	Depressed individual or extremely organized
Bar in middle of stem	Careful, cautious, methodical, not spontaneous
Bar on top of stem	Impractical daydreamer
Bar connected to next letter	Quick mind and intelligent
Bar to right of stem	Impatient, driven, goal-oriented, energetic and ambitious
Bar to left of stem	Cautious, has a hard time making decisions
Downward sloping bar	Anger, tension, stress
Upward sloping bar	Optimistic, happy, carefree

Rounded bar	Sensitive, needs affection and security
Bar long and thin	Protective, patronizing, low tolerance levels
Angular bar	Irritable, cross and short-tempered
Heavy bar	Thoughtful
Light bar	Sensitive
Knots in bar	Private person who is thorough
Hooks in bar	Does not leave a job half done, sees it through to the end
Sharp end on beginning of bar	Quick temper
Sharp end on end of bar	Slow to anger

Spacing

Spacing refers to the area between the letters and words and between each line of text in a handwriting sample. Some people write with the letters practically on top of each other and with the words and lines of text close together. Others write with the letters and words equally far apart and the same amount of space between the lines. Still others put additional space between each of these components. When you are evaluating spacing you should do so in conjunction with the other facets of the analysis.

You can think of spacing in terms of normal and abnormal. In graphology normal spacing has equal amounts of space between each word, which means that the writer is emotionally stable and balanced. Abnormal spacing is often irregular and has poor or unusual amounts of space between words, which indicates that the person can be emotionally unstable and follows her impulses. The amount of space that the writer does or does not place between words also tells the graphologist about her social behavior.

Evaluating space is something that comes

with practice. The text should look as if it has a good smooth flow to it even if the spacing between words seems to be a little wide or narrow. If the flow with the rest of the sample is consistent with the overall writing style, then this would be considered a good flow.

Consider these two examples.

A. *Someday I want to go to the moon.*

B. *Is this your book? May I have it?*

Look at example A. In this writing sample there is an equal amount of space between each word. This means that the person gets along well with others and is well balanced in relationships. Now imagine that all the words in example A were right on top of each other, making it difficult to distinguish one word from the next with little or no space between them. If you see that kind of writing then it indicates someone who may not have a clear understanding of social boundaries or who feels she needs to be close to others. An example might be someone who invades your personal space while talking to you or someone who is constantly touching your arm or shoulder during a conversation. Writing with little or no spacing is also indicative of high levels of stress.

Now look at example B. The additional spacing between the words "your book" and "I have" can indicate that the writer is lonely and that she does not feel close to others. When the spacing is wide she tends to be more laid-back and open-minded than someone who uses less space.

Margins

Margins are the borders that writers instinctively create as they write on a blank sheet of paper. We will take a look at what some of the common margins mean to a graphologist.

The most prevalent uses of margin are those that are equal in nature, meaning that the writer has left as much space on the top and bottom as on the sides. Imagine a printed document with one-inch margins all the way around. When a person naturally writes with these equal margins, it shows that she likes her life, is comfortable in her own skin, is balanced, organized and efficient, both on a personal level and in her career.

If a writer leaves wide right-hand margins she tends to be rather serious with only a few close friends. She is apprehensive and does not trust people easily. She tends to stay away from crowded places and prefers to be alone.

In the case of a writer who leaves wide bottom margins, she is afraid of emotions, her own and those of others. She has a fear of being hurt, even if it is an unfounded fear and she has never been emotionally hurt before. She tends to think, "What if?" and imagines the worst possible scenario without reason. On the other hand, she can be a good listener, as long as she does not let herself get involved on an emotional level and she tends to be quite perceptive.

What does it mean when the writer starts writing partway down the page instead of near the top, thereby leaving a wide top margin? She tends to be very laid-back. She does not like making decisions and would rather leave it to someone else. This may not be due to a lack of responsibility but instead a lack of confidence.

Narrow margins have different meanings depending on which margins are narrow. If all four margins are narrow, this indicates someone who is extroverted with good people skills. If the top margin is narrow she tends to be very direct and goes after what she wants in life. If the left margin is narrow she is cautious and afraid of making mistakes. No margins at all indicate thriftiness and a tendency to be obsessive about holding onto possessions.

Irregular margins symbolize someone who can be both an extrovert and withdrawn while keeping to herself.

Envelopes

Envelopes are an important part of handwriting analysis that is sometimes overlooked. Consider the envelope as the public display of personality (similar to a signature) and the letter inside the envelope as the private person.

When analyzing an envelope, you will want to divide it into four quadrants by folding it in half both vertically and then horizontally. The address should be centered and start about halfway down the envelope. If it is in the correct place then the writer has a good understanding of how to complete an envelope, has good judgment and is a balanced person. If the address is primarily in the upper left quadrant, then she is a daydreamer who is emotional and easily influenced. If it is in the lower left quadrant she is materialistic. If it is in the upper right quadrant, she is affectionate and impulsive. The address in the lower right quadrant indicates she is realistic with a sense of adventure. If the address is placed high on the envelope then she is careless.

Large writing is typical of an extrovert, while small writing is typical of an introvert.

Illegible writing shows an individual who could care less about what others think of her and who does not have respect for authority.

It is important to compare the writing on the envelope with the writing on the letter contained inside. Sometimes you will find contradictions between the two and other times there will be information inside that confirms the initial data obtained from the envelope. If someone uses large writing on the envelope but small writing in the letter, she is trying to impress the recipient. If the opposite is true, she may feel modest or is trying to appear less than she really is. Handwriting on the letter and the envelope that matches means she is balanced. When the writing is indented, as in the delivery address in the example below, it shows she is overly cautious and may have inhibitions.

JANE DOE
PO Box 1154
ANYWHERE   USA 00258

JOHN SMITH
PO Box 5624
ANYWHERE USA 66597

Signatures

There are several different types of signatures that graphologists consider when doing the analysis. Signatures reveal information that may not be apparent in other text. Think of the signature as the writer acting on their best behavior. It is the public image that is being presented to the world and may be plain, ornate or have simple lines.

Can signatures change? Yes. Any time you have gone through transformations in your life or in your manner of thinking it can be reflected in your signature. It could be a minor change or a complete overhaul, depending on how extreme the transformation was that you experienced.

Here are some different types of signatures and their meanings. I have used the same name written with the different strokes so that you can easily distinguish the different elements used when creating signatures.

Underlined signatures mean that the writer is emphasizing her name because she is proud of herself and her accomplishments in life. She feels that she needs to make an impression on the reader. The underline may be thin, thick, long or short. Regardless of its shape, the underlining of a signature is an indication of self-importance and self-emphasis. Any type of underlining is the writer's way to make a bold statement about herself.

A rounded signature shows that the writer is honest, reliable and dependable. This is the person you can count on when life gets out of balance. She is the one who will tell you the truth no matter how much you do not want to hear it but she will do it gently and with love. She is caring and considers the feelings of others in all that she does. She is friendly, communicates easily with others, likes to participate in social events and quite often acts as a volunteer. She is trustworthy and well-liked.

Julie Smith

Does the signature slant upwards? Then the author is ambitious and filled with hope. This is a goal oriented person who works hard to accomplish her dreams. She is organized, efficient and thrives on planning her own success. This does not mean that she is conceited but instead indicates that she knows what she wants and takes the steps to ensure that she gets it. She is very positive and upbeat, inspiring those around her to reach their fullest potential.

Julie Smith

An encircled signature suggests that the writer feels fear and has a difficult time facing the world so she protects her signature, thus protecting herself, by encircling it. This can reveal tendencies toward depression. A covering stroke of this nature can also indicate that she is trying to hide something in her life from others. In the example below you will see that the encircling stroke covers both the first and last names. Some people also use strokes that only cover their last name or they may even cover each section of their name individually with a separate covering stroke for the first name and another one for the last name.

Embellished signatures that have a lot of extraneous decoration, loops, swirls and squiggles show someone who needs attention and is trying to gain it through flamboyant writing. The person with an embellished signature often seeks attention through her actions in her daily life. She is usually an extrovert who may also feel slightly inferior but covers it up by being extremely outgoing, a little on the loud side, and may even use large hand gestures when talking in order to draw attention to herself. She feels she deserves attention and gives it to herself when creating a signature.

The way a person writes her first and last name can reveal a lot. A larger first name and smaller surname indicates that she may not be too thrilled with the members of her family. Someone in the family may have caused her pain, disappointments or neglected her. In turn, she writes the surname smaller to place as little value on it as possible. Sometimes a larger first name simply indicates that the person wishes to be called by her given name.

A larger last name means that she is proud of her family, her heritage and holds family in high regard. When she includes her middle name or initial that shows that she is full of pride (unless it is being used as a formality). If the first initial of the last name is taller than the other letters (as in the first example below) this indicates an honor of hearth and home. Deep respect for traditional family ways and tradition are important to her.

Does the signature slant downward? That is suggestive of discouragement or depression. It could be temporary or a sign of more serious mental conditions. When times are hard, work is not going well and nerves are frayed, you may see a downward sloping signature. Make sure you compare it to the rest of the text. If you notice that the majority of the text is without a downward slope then this shows that the discouragement she is feeling is evident only in her signature, the most personal part of the text. If the entire text has a downward slant as well as the signature, then it could be indicative of a more serious problem.

Strikes from the end of the signature back through the name are a writer's way of canceling themselves out. A divorced woman who kept her previous last name for her children may cross through the last name because of ill feelings toward her ex-husband. A child who dislikes her father may also cross out her last name. You will usually find this crossing out through part or all of the name is based on negative feelings toward family. When the person is able to release these negative feelings, or is able to change their name through marriage or the court system, the signature usually changes and lacks the backward slash that cancelled out the name.

A small signature shows that the person is inhibited, feels a need for protection and is afraid to get hurt. The smaller the space between each letter and the smaller the height of the signature, the more these three characteristics apply. A small signature suggests someone who pulls away from society and prefers being alone to having the attention of others. She may feel that she does not fit in anywhere and that she is different from everyone else that she meets. In the past she may have been hurt by someone and withdraws so that it will never happen again.

When analyzing a signature always try to do it in comparison to the text that the person wrote above the signature. If the signature is smaller than the text then it suggests inhibitions or wanting to appear inhibited. If the signature is larger, the opposite is true. She wants to appear more than she is, bigger than life and impressive. You may also find a person using more than one signature. For example, she may use a small signature for private documents but a larger more elaborate signature for everyday use. Our signatures can also change during our lives. The overall shape may stay basically the same but nuances caused by life events can be added to or deleted from the signature.

Doodling

Some people doodle, some do not. Unlike writing, which takes a conscious effort to do, doodling occurs at a more subconscious level. A doodle is the brain's way of expressing itself when you are concentrating on something else. Many artistic people doodle while those who don't think in pictures may not.

If you are a doodler, how many times have you been on the phone, engrossed in a conversation, only to hang up and notice that you have a page full of doodles? Have you ever stopped to look at them and decide what they mean? Once you have gotten a taste of graphology, you will find that you want to analyze those funny little pictures and graphics that you have created when your thoughts were elsewhere.

Doodles are an excellent way to analyze a writer's personality and character through an unconscious action. Sometimes the designs are repetitive and other times they are not. The graphics drawn give key insights so let us consider some interpretations of different types of doodles.

Doodles are usually characterized in two ways—abstract or recognizable. An example of an abstract doodle could be circles with triangles inside surrounded by a spiral. A recognizable doodle would be a refrigerator drawn when someone was hungry. Here's a list of some of the most common doodles and their meanings.

Arrows	Ambitious and motivated feelings, driven to succeed
Boxes	A desire to be constructive, three dimensional boxes indicate the ability to look at situations from all sides
Circles	Independence, passive feelings, being social, flexible, loving and friendly, talkative

Clouds	Escapism and deep emotions, filled in clouds suggest the writer is having a hard time coping
Faces	Frequently show the mood of the doodler
Flowers	Show the feminine side of the writer (even if the writer is male)
Food	A need for love, thirst, hunger, a desire to be filled emotionally or physically
Hearts	Indicates someone in love or thinking about love and romance
Houses	Houses that include windows, doors and landscaping show that the doodler is happy with their home life, houses that appear unadorned and are drawn in an off-centered manner indicate problems at home
Lines, Mazes	Inner conflict, lines that go in all directions without any specific shape or form indicate that the person is without direction and purpose
Name	Doodling one's own name over and over shows a large ego,

	doodles around a name show a need for protecting the person whose name was written
Numbers	Money problems, when the money sign is included with the numbers then it indicates severe money problems
Stars	Hopefulness, optimistic, feelings of excitement toward the future, looking forward to things in life
Trees	Trees with lots of branches show a thinker, trees with a large base show a physical person, trees with fruit show love of family
Triangles	Wanting a resolution to a problem, realistic feelings, problem solver looking for a resolution
Vehicles	A need to escape or boredom with one's job, family or life

Doodles of death and destruction or doodling on inappropriate things (walls, books and so on) show an unhappy person who needs to be heard, seen and loved. Organized doodles, which appear in a row, are detailed, well-balanced and symmetrical or placing similar doodles in their own section on the page show the person is law-abiding and constructive.

Composing Your Analysis

Now that you understand the basics of handwriting analysis, it is time to create the actual analysis. This is the fun part that brings it all together. You never know when you will need to access this information so stick this little book in your backpack or purse so it will always be at your fingertips for quick reference.

Make sure that you have already obtained your handwriting sample and have it in front of you before you start. Begin by jotting down notes about the sample. When you are doing the analysis, you should make sure that you have several indicators that all point to the same characteristic prior to stating that the characteristic is part of the person. For example, if you see one indicator suggesting that the person is highly excitable you should not say this unless you found other indicators within the text to back up the statement. Then, when you reveal this knowledge, you should do so in a professional manner and with tact. With practice, you will soon develop your own style of creating and delivering the analysis.

After you have taken a lot of notes during

your analysis, organize these notes and compose them into a clear flowing report that logically moves from one area to the next. You may even create your own worksheet of notes prior to writing up the analysis so that they will be organized and easy to follow. Here is an example of some subjects that you will want to include on your worksheet. You may choose to have a small section for each topic or a whole page—the layout is completely up to you and dependent upon the amount of detail you are including under each topic heading.

NAME:	AGE:	GENDER:
Trait	*Specifics*	*Meaning*
Baseline:		
Spacing:		
Zones:		
Margins:		
Connections:		
Legibility:		
Size:		
Rhythm:		
Strokes:		
Lettering Size:		
Form:		

Speed:		
Slant:		
Numbers:		
Lower Case t:		
i-dots:		
Pressure:		
Envelopes:		
Loops:		
Type:		
Signatures:		
Doodles:		
Punctuation:		
Overall Impressions:		
Conclusion:		

If you are doing the analysis for someone else you can also deliver the information verbally instead of a through a written analysis, either directly in a one-on-one meeting or you can record it and give them the tape. Or you could provide both a written and oral/taped delivery.

There are also several things you should stay away from as you put together your final analysis. You do not want to diagnose mental illness or physical problems unless you are also a doctor who practices medicine, a psychologist or you have a medical license to offer such diagnoses.

Inevitably you will miss some things within an analysis or get something wrong. That is completely normal and acceptable. Even when we do the best job that we can do, humans are not perfect so do not expect to be one hundred percent right all of the time. As a seer, I tell my clients the exact same thing. No clairvoyant is one hundred percent accurate and, if they say they are, then you should not get a reading from them. If a graphologist tells you they are one hundred percent accurate then I would say to stay away from that person's business too. It is easy to be hard on yourself if you miss something in an analysis but try to give yourself the understanding that you would offer to others.

One thing that you always want to remember is that you must hold yourself accountable for your analysis. If you are not sure about something, or you feel a niggling sense that you should not include something for whatever reason, then follow your gut feelings. Intuition is helpful in doing an analysis. Do not put something in the analysis that can come back and bite you later.

The Business of Graphology

Can you make a career as a graphologist? If you want to take your love of handwriting analysis to the next level and make it a consulting business, there are several steps you must take to ensure success.

Before you launch into a business of analyzing handwriting make sure you have the knowledge that you will need to be successful. Gather your tools—a ruler with millimeters, a protractor, a magnifying glass and a copybook such as the Palmer, Zaner-Bloser or the D'Nealian standards.

You will have to study and practice until you are comfortable with detecting all of the variations that occur in handwriting analysis. You can also take courses or workshops in graphology and take a psychology or writing class. All of these will help you with the final composition of your analysis. Sink yourself into the craft of graphology until you feel comfortable that you know what you are doing and can offer your clients a quality handwriting analysis. Only start working on a professional basis when you feel comfortable with your skill level. You will also need to make sales and market your services so brush up on ways to do that effectively.

Just as in any field, you will need to follow ethical practices and legalities so that you build a solid reputation as a professional graphology consulting business. Start a company and operate within the state and local laws in your area. Do you need a business license or will you have to file certain types of taxes? Get all of these requirements in place before you launch your business so it is set up correctly in the beginning.

There are numerous places where you can use your graphology skills. One of the most popular places to obtain employment is within human resources departments of major corporations. Graphology is also used in recruitment, at corporate events. Graphologists are also used in criminal profiling and forensic science. You can also sell your services on the web to people who are just curious about what their handwriting says about them. The possibilities are unlimited. Whenever there is a need to know more about a person, graphology is a useful tool.

Conclusion

I hope this book has given you insights into, and whetted your appetite for, the art of handwriting analysis, also called graphology. It is really an intriguing way to learn more about others, especially when they are people that you are going to be involved with on a daily basis. When you are doing your analysis refer to the details in this book often and soon it will become second nature. Whether you decide to pursue graphology as a hobby or as a full-time career, I wish you much success.

Bibliography

Handwriting Analysis by P. Scott Hollander, Llewellyn Publications, St. Paul, MN, 1991.

Handwriting Analysis, Putting It To Work For You by Andrea McNichol and Jeffery A. Nelson, NTC/Contemporary Publishing Group, Chicago, IL, 1991.

Idiot's Guide to Handwriting Analysis, The by Sheila Lowe, Penguin Group, New York, NY, 2007.

Manual of Graphology edited by Peter West, Quantum, Cippenham, Slough, Berks, England, 1999.

Signature for Success by Arlyn Imberman, Andrews McMeel Publishing, Kansas City, MO, 2003.

Simply Handwriting Analysis by Eve Bingham, Sterling Publishing Co., New York, NY, 2007.

MELISSA ALVAREZ

BIO

Melissa Alvarez is a multi-published, award-winning author who writes nonfiction under her real name and paranormal romantic suspense under the pen name Ariana Dupré. She is also an internationally known clairvoyant advisor and does readings from her site at apsychichaven.com. She owns Friesian horses and German Shepherds with her husband and together they are successful breeders of champions. She enjoys reading and spending time with her family, horses and dogs when she's not writing. Melissa lives in sunny South Florida where the weather is wonderful unless a hurricane is on the horizon. Visit her online at www.MelissaA.com for updates on new releases, contests and a plethora of articles.

LaVergne, TN USA
21 December 2010
209704LV00001B/70/P